DK Watch me grow

Turtle

LONDON, NEW YORK, MUNICH,
MELBOURNE, and DELHI

Written and edited by Lisa Magloff
Design and digital artworking by Sonia Moore
DTP designer Almudena Díaz
Picture researcher Suzanne Williams
Production Lucy Baker

Publishing managers Susan Leonard and
Joanne Connor

First published in Great Britain in 2006 by
Dorling Kindersley Limited
80 Strand, London WC2R 0RL

A Penguin Company

Copyright © 2006 Dorling Kindersley Limited, London

A CIP catalogue record for this book
is available from the British Library.

ISBN-13 978-1-4053-1309-4
ISBN-10 1-4053-1309-9

Hi-res workflow proofed by
Media, Development and Printing, Ltd, Great Britain
Digital artworking by Sonia Moore
Printed and bound in China by South China Printing Co. Ltd

Discover more at

www.dk.com

Contents

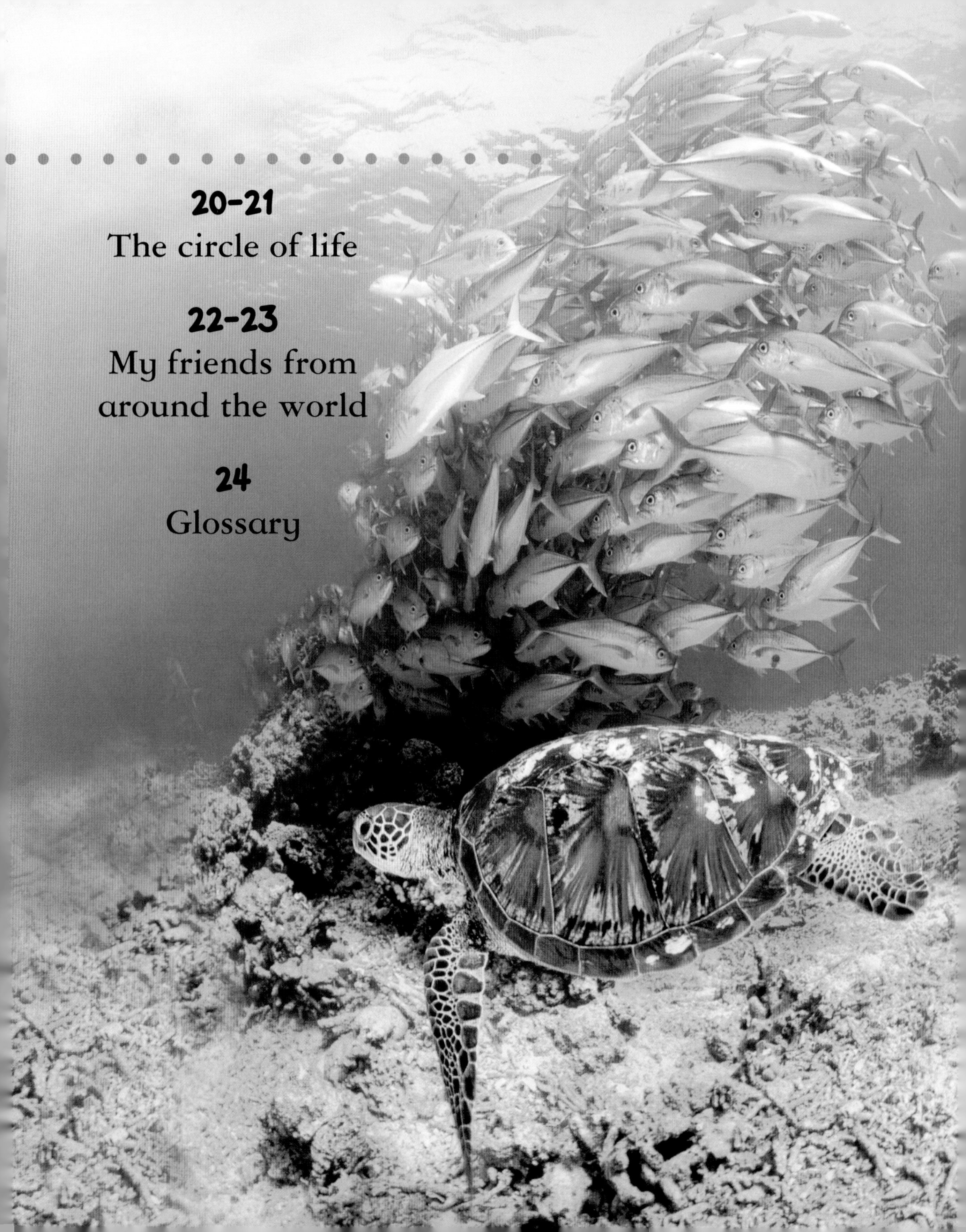

I'm a green sea turtle

I'm a green sea turtle. I swim in the ocean, but I come to the surface to breathe air. I eat plants and small animals from the sea and spend most of my life under the water with my friends.

A hard shell covers the turtle's back and chest.

The flippers are covered in tough scales.

The turtle's eyes are protected by thick eyelids.

Turtles breathe air through two nostrils, just like us!

I live in oceans all over the world.

Sea turtles tear their food with a sharp beak.

Soft, bendy skin allows the turtle's head and flippers to move.

My mum and dad

My mum and dad met while swimming in the sea. After mating, Mum will lay four or five nests full of eggs. She will lay one nest every two weeks.

The male turtle uses his fippers to hold on to the female.

This is my dad.

This is my mum.

After mating, the turtles do not stay together.

Swimming to shore

Sea turtles can travel hundreds or thousands of miles from the place where they live to the place where they mate and lay eggs.

Heave ho, up we go...

The female turtle uses her strong front flippers to drag herself out of the water and on to the sand. It's hard work and she usually waits until morning or night time, when it's cool.

Mum buries her eggs

My mum crawls up on to the sand to lay her eggs. She digs a hole and lays them one at a time. Our eggs have soft shells so they do not break when they fall. The sandy nest will protect us and keep us warm.

Safe and sound

After laying the eggs, the turtle covers them with sand using her back flippers. Turtles lay their eggs on the same beach every year.

Digging and laying eggs is hard work. It can take the turtle a few hours to dig the nest and lay the eggs.

Mum's powerful flippers flick and fling the sand away.

The nest will be big enough to hold between 60 and 120 eggs.

It's time to hatch out

After two months under the sand, we hatch out of our shells. Once everyone has hatched, we all work together to dig to the surface.

Digging through the sand is very hard work. It can take the turtles a whole week to dig to the surface.

Let's get digging.

This crab can feel something moving under the sand. Hurry up turtles – he's starting to dig for his dinner!

Turtle facts

. . . .

The turtles use a tiny, hard tooth, called an egg tooth, to help them break open their shell.

The baby sea turtles are about 5 cm (2 in) long.

If the temperature in the nest is hot, all the hatchlings will be girls. If it is cooler, they will all be boys!

I'm off to the sea

My brothers and sisters and I work together to dig our way to the surface.
Then we all rush for the sea.
Once we are in the water, we all swim away.

Hurry up! It's safer in the sea, let's get there as quick as we can.

On land, birds, lizards, and other animals will try to catch the baby turtles.

The hatchlings wait until it's cool to run for the sea.

The hatchlings all leave their nest at the same time, for safety.

Seaweed hide and seek

Now that I am in the ocean,
I stay safe by hiding in the
seaweed. This will be my home
until I am bigger. I eat small animals
that live in the seaweed.

The turtles will spend
many years floating
on seaweed.

Turtle treats

· · · · · · · · · · · · · · · · ·

Adult sea turtles eat mainly sea-grasses that grow deeper down, but baby sea turtles eat all sorts of tiny animals that live near the surface. These are called plankton. Jellyfish and sponges also make a tasty treat for the young turtles.

Plankton

This turtle is two months old. She stays close to the surface so she can breathe.

It's time to get clean

As I grow bigger and swim around more, my shell gets covered in algae. Algae is not good for me, so I need to keep clean. My friends and I line up and wait for fish to eat up all the algae on our shells.

At the cleaning station, the fish get food, and the turtles get cleaned.

All clean... See you later guys.

Sometimes cleaning only takes a few minutes – other times it can take hours.

Cleaning facts

The algae on the turtles' shells slows them down in the water and can cause illness.

At the cleaning station, the turtles stretch out so the fish can reach every spot.

Sometimes shrimp also help with the cleaning.

I'm a big turtle now

I'm 15 years old. I'm finally big enough to swim anywhere in the ocean on my own. Most of the time I like to stay close to land, where there is a lot of food to eat.

Sea turtles are very strong swimmers.

Sea turtles need to surface for air.

Underwater life

Adult sea turtles can stay under water for up to five hours before taking a breath of air.

Eat your greens

Adult sea turtles eat only plants. They eat seaweed, sea grass, and algae. They spend most of their time looking for food in shallow areas of the sea.

This turtle is looking for a rock cave to sleep in.

The circle of life goes round and round

Now you know how I turned into a grown-up sea turtle.

My friends from around the world

Some of my friends live in freshwater rivers and lakes and some live in the salty ocean with me. But we are all turtles.

Snake-necked turtles live in fresh water rivers all over Australia.

I'm a Leatherback turtle.

Hawksbill turtles live in warm seas all around the world.

Alligator snapping turtles eat fish and live in rivers in the southern part of the United States of America.

The Olive Ridley turtle lives in the sea and gets its name from its green shell.

I'm a young Loggerhead turtle.

Leatherback turtles live in the ocean and can grow as big as a small car.

Turtle facts

🐢 The Green sea turtle gets its name from the colour of its body fat, which is green from the algae it eats.

🐢 Sea turtles can live to be more than 80 years old.

🐢 Instead of a hard shell, the Leatherback has a thick skin that is supported by bones.

Glossary

Flipper
The turtle's arm. It is flat and shaped for swimming.

Hatch
When the baby sea turtle pecks its way out of its egg.

Beak
The hard upper part of the turtle's mouth, used for eating.

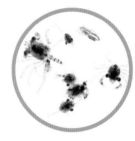

Plankton
Tiny sea animals that are food for the adult sea turtle.

Scales
Hard, flat plates that make up the turtle's shell and skin.

Reef
A hard ridge made up of coral, rocks, and sand.

Acknowledgements
The publisher would like to thank the following for their kind permission to reproduce their photographs:
(Key: a=above; c=centre; b=below; l=left; r=right; t=top)
1 SeaPics: James D.Watt. 2-3: SeaPics: Doug Perrine. 4-5 Alamy: Carlos Villoch. 4 Oxford Scientific Films: Gerard Soury tl; Alamy: Carlos Villoch bl. 5 Oxford Scientific Films cr. 6 Nature Photo Library: Doug Perrine. 7: Getty Images: David Fleetham t; Jim Angy b. 8: Science Photo Library: Alexis Rosenfeld l. 9 Getty Images: Cousteau Society. 10-11 James L. Amos. 10 Alamy: Aqua Image c; Image Quest Marine: Tim Hellier bl; Still Pictures: Kevin Aitkin ctr. 11 Corbis: Kevin Schafer cl; Getty Images: Tim Laman tr; Natural Visions: Soames Summerhays br. 12 Frank Lane Picture Agency: Frans Lanting/Minden Pictures bl; SeaPics: Doug Perrine tl; NHPA: B. Jones & M.Shimlock. 14-15 Getty Images: Bill Curtsinger. 15 Science Photo Library: Alexis Rosenfeld tr. 16 Getty Images: A Witte/C Mahaney b; Oxford Scientific Films: Photolibrary tl.

17 Maui Sea Life: Doug & Kerry Pilot. 18-19 Getty Images: Jeff Hunter. 18 Getty Images: Michael Gilbert tl. 19 Oxford Scientific Films: Photolibrary br; SeaPics: Doug Perrine t. 20 Alamy: M. Timothy O'Keefe bl; Alamy: Aqua Image crb; Corbis: Kevin Schafer cra; Image Quest Marine tc & tcr; Image Quest Marine: James D. Watt clb; Natural Visions: Soames Summerhays crbb; NHPA: Linda Pitkin cl; Oxford Scientific Films/Photolibrary: Gerard Soury bc; Science Photo Library: Alexis Rosenfeld c; Lumigenic: Mark Shargel tl. 21 Oxford Scientific Films/Photolibrary. 22-23 Still Pictures: Kelvin Aitken cb. 22 Alamy: Michael Patrick O'Neill bl. 23 Alamy: CuboImages srl; Alfio Giannotti rc; NHPA: Martin Wendler tr. 24 Alamy: Carlos Villoch bl; Corbis: Kevin Schafer tr; Getty Images: Jeff Hunter br; Oxford Scientific Films/Photolibrary cl; SeaPics: James D. Watt tl.
All other images © Dorling Kindersley
For further information see: www.dkimages.com